THE POETRY
OF WALT WHITMAN

By

WILLIAM LYON PHELPS

First published in 1924

British Library Cataloguing-in-Publication Data
A catalogue record for this book is available
from the British Library

CONTENTS

Walt Whitman

Walt Whitman was born on 31st May 1819 in the Town of Huntington, Long Island, New York, USA. He was the second of nine children of Walter Whitman and Louisa Van Velsor Whitman. In part due to a series of bad investments, the family lived in various homes in the Brooklyn area, and Whitman recalled his childhood as generally restless and unhappy, given his family's difficult economic status. Whitman finished his formal schooling at age eleven, and immediately sought employment to aid his family. He worked in an office of a legal firm and later as an apprentice and printer's devil for the weekly Long Island newspaper, the *Patriot*. The following summer, Whitman took a job with the leading Whig newspaper the *Long-Island Star*, and it was here that he developed a strong interest in reading, writing and theatre. He also anonymously published some of his earliest poetry in the *New York Mirror*.

After a brief sojourn as a teacher, living back with his family in Long Island, Whitman returned to New York to establish his own newspaper; the *Long Islander*. He embarked on this project in the spring of 1838, but sold the paper to E.O. Crowell after only ten months. From 1840-41 Whitman attempted to further his career in teaching, but with little success, he returned to writing. During this time, Whitman published a series of ten editorials, called *Sun-Down Papers—From the Desk of a Schoolmaster*, in three newspapers between the winter of 1840 and July 1841. In these essays, he adopted a constructed persona, a technique he would employ throughout his career. It was not until 1850 that Whitman began writing what would later become *Leaves of Grass*; a collection of poetry which he continued editing and revising until his death. The first edition was a success, and stirred up significant interest, partly due to the praise it received by Ralph Waldo Emerson. However the volume, which Whitman intended as 'a distinctly American epic', attracted substantial criticism for its 'offensive' and 'crude' sexual themes. It deviated from the historic use of an elevated hero and instead assumed the identity of the common person; part of the transition in American literature, moving away from transcendentalism towards realism. In light of the contemporary criticism, Whitman's sexuality is often discussed alongside his poetry. Though biographers continue to debate his sexuality, he is usually described as either homosexual or bisexual - yet this remains speculation.

Whitman lived through the American Civil war, and volunteered as a nurse in army hospital, later serving as a clerk in the *Bureau of Indian Affairs* in the Department of the Interior. In June of 1865, Whitman was fired from his job – most likely on moral grounds, by the former Iowa Senator James Harlan, after he found an 1860 edition of *Leaves of Grass*. Whitman's friend William Douglas O'Connor, a well-connected poet and newspaper editor was incensed by this iniquitousness, and wrote a pamphlet defending Whitman as a wholesome patriot, greatly increasing his popularity. Further adding to Whitman's fame during this period was the publication of *O Captain! My Captain!*; a relatively conventional poem chronicling the death of Abraham Lincoln. It was the only poem to appear in anthologies during Whitman's lifetime. The author then moved onto work at the Attorney General's office, interviewing former Confederate soldiers for Presidential Pardons - an occupation which was more to Whitman's taste. He later wrote to a friend; 'there are real characters among them... and you know I have a fancy for anything out of the ordinary.' During this time, Whitman succeeded in finding a publisher for *Leaves of Grass* (eventually issued in 1871), the same year it was mistakenly reported that its author died in a railroad accident. Only two years after this great personal success, Whitman suffered a paralytic stroke (early in 1873) and was induced to move to the home of his brother in

New Jersey. Whilst there, he was very productive, publishing three versions of *Leaves of Grass*, as well as other works. This was also the last point at which Whitman was fully mobile, and he received many famous authors, including Oscar Wilde and Thomas Eakins. In 1884, he bought his own house, remaining in New Jersey, but became completely bedridden soon after. In the last week of his life, Whitman was too weak even to lift a knife or fork, and wrote; 'I suffer all the time: I have no relief, no escape: it is monotony—monotony—monotony—in pain.' He died from diminished lung capacity, the result of bronchial pneumonia and an abscess on the chest, on 26 March 1892.

By the time of his death, Whitman had become a veritable national celebrity, and a public viewing of his body was held at his home; an event which attracted over one thousand people in three hours. His coffin was barely visible because of all the flowers and wreaths. Whitman was buried four days later at Harleigh Cemetery in Camden, New Jersey. He has since been eulogised as America's first 'poet of democracy', due to his uncanny ability to write in the American character, and remains an enduring and much loved literary figure to this day.

EDITOR'S NOTE

THE material contained in this book is a reprint of the second essay in the volume by William Lyon Phelps, entitled "*Howells, James, Bryant and Other Essays.*"

The Poetry of Walt Whitman looking over some Whitman manuscripts in the library of Yale University, I found a letter from the poet, which is so characteristic that I place it here at the head of this essay

THE POETRY OF WALT WHITMAN

Camden, Oct. 14, 1880.

Dear Tom: I got home all safe -We stopped a day & a night at Niagara & had a first rate time-- Started the next morning early in an easy comfortable palace car & went on like a streak through New York & Pennsylvania-got into Philadelphia after 11 at night- (we were an hour late) -but the city looked bright & all alive. O I felt as fresh as a lark-I am well, my summer in Canada has done me great good-it is not only the fine country & climate there, but I found such good friends, good quarters, good grub, & everything that could make a man happy-The last five days I have been down on a jaunt to the sea-shore. . . I sat hours enjoying it, for it suits me-I was born & brought up near the sea, & I could listen forever to the hoarse music of the surf-Tom I got your paper & handbill, good for you, boy-believe me I was pleased to know you won.

Whitman was always cheerful, always the optimist, always the affirmer of life, and the believer in it. He regarded mere animal existence as a huge asset, and conscious living as a continuous joy. He had as little of Mark Twain's pessimism as of his humour; the only point where these representative Americans came in contact was their faith in the universal principle of Democracy.

Who is America's foremost poet? It would be impossible to obtain a majority on a secret ballot for any one. Poe, Emerson, Longfellow, Whittier, Lowell, Whitman have many supporters. Our most popular poet is of course Longfellow; but the greatest? I cannot tell. Emerson and Whitman are the most unconventional, the most free of tradition.

John Burroughs, the faithful disciple of old Walt, divided all poets into two classes-Primary and Secondary. He declared emphatically that Whitman was a greater poet than Tennyson, because Tennyson was a secondary man, and Whitman was primary. He meant that Tennyson followed in broad highways, whereas Whitman blazed a trail. However this may be, I do not believe that Whitman was a greater poet than Tennyson, for the simple reason that his poetry is not so good as Tennyson's.

Yet the reputation of Walt Whitman was never so high as it is now. There were two American centenaries in the year 1919; homage was paid to Lowell and to Whitman. But the latter poet was more widely and more vigorously applauded. There are still many sceptics, many avowed antagonists; but we shall never be rid of him. We cannot say, as some tried to say of a greater poet with the same initials, William Wordsworth,

Here lies W. W.

Who no more will trouble you, trouble you,

for Whitman will trouble us to the end of our lives, and cannot be dismissed with a Podsnappian gesture.

The history of his reputation demands a volume by itself. It began with *Leaves of Grass*, in 1855. That was a notable year in poetry, for it saw also the appearance of Tennyson's *Maud*, Browning's *Men and Women*, Longfellow's *Hiawatha*. *Maud* and *Hiawatha* received much ridicule, and *Men and Women* received silence. Today all these poems are very much alive.

Whitman's admiration of other poets was sufficiently eclectic. His roll-call of the "mighty ones" is as follows: Job, Homer, Aeschylus, Dante, Shakespeare, Tennyson, Emerson.

What I shall say about Whitman will please nobody; for I am neither among the worshippers nor the scorners. To me he is neither one-of-the-greatest-poets-of-all-time nor is he a charlatan. I refuse to become excited or polemical in this matter. Whitman needs no defence and attacks cannot hurt him.

It was during the 'seventies that the battle raged most fiercely. To some enthusiasts, Whitman was in the front row with Homer and Shakespeare; to other men he was an unclean boor who should be summarily expelled into the outer darkness. Just when the fight was hottest, an obscure young Scot by the name of Robert Louis Stevenson published an essay called *The Gospel According to Walt Whitman* (1878) which in 1923 seems still to be the best appraisal. Let me quote the first paragraph

> Of late years the name of Walt Whitman has been a good deal bandied about in books and magazines. It has become familiar both in good and ill repute. His works have been largely bespattered with praise by his admirers, and cruelly mauled and mangled by irreverent enemies. Now, whether his poetry is good or bad as poetry, is a matter that may admit of a difference of opinion without alienating those who differ. We could not keep the peace with a man who should put forward claims to taste and yet depreciate the choruses in Samson Agonistes; but I think we may shake hands with one who sees no more in Walt Whitman's volume from a literary point of view, than a farrago of incompetent essays in a wrong direction. That may not be at all our own opinion. We may think that, when a work contains so many unforgettable phrases, it cannot be altogether devoid of literary merit. We may even see passages of a high poetry here and there among its eccentric contents. But when all is said, Walt Whitman is neither a Milton nor a Shakespeare; to appreciate his works is not a condition necessary to salvation; and I would not disinherit a son upon the question, nor even think much the worse of a critic, for I should always have an idea what he meant.

Whitman was born on a farm in Long Island, 31 May 1819. He was the second of nine children, and was called "Walt" to distinguish him from his father Walter. He was the only one of the brood to show any ability. Bliss Perry says the oldest died a lunatic and the youngest was an imbecile.

When he was four years old, the family moved to Brooklyn. Walt had little formal education; at the age of 13, he left school "for good." He did much desultory reading, set type in a printing office, did editorial writing on the *Brooklyn Eagle*, and taught school. This last experience he valued highly. The best thing he got out of his newspaper work was free admission to the New York theatres; he was a constant attendant at plays and operas. Like most men of force and vigour, he loved to read the Bible, and was particularly fond of reading it outdoors, which is one of the severest tests that can be applied to any book. He knocked around the South as a jolly vagabond, doing odd jobs in New Orleans and other places. During the Civil War, he did noble and devoted service in taking care of the sick and wounded in the hospitals. He had everlasting patience, reading to the men, and writing letters for them, listening to their talk and telling them stories. In 1873 paralysis seized him. His declining years were spent at Camden, New Jersey. Friends supported him, and he thoroughly enjoyed life, sending copies of his own books to purchasers, composing and revising, receiving daily visits from idolaters and pilgrims who came from everywhere. He became a Sage, and his particular Boswell, Horace Traubel, has left a voluminous and detailed record of his conversations. He died on 26 March 1892. All of Whitman's unconventionalities, in dress, name, and literary style, were deliberately assumed. They were not spontaneous. As a young man, he was something of a macaroni. He dressed in formal and elaborate style, with a frock coat, tall silk hat, and carried a cane. Later he wore a grey flannel shirt, open at the neck, with rolling Byronic collar. In each case he meant to be conspicuous, and succeeded. Originally he signed his work Walter Whitman, and later changed to Walt, as more free-

and-easy. His literary career began in an extremely conventional manner; his first publications were in prose, his enemies insist that his later ones were also. When he wrote his first poems, they were written in a correct, conventional, traditional, uninspired metrical form. Probably no famous writer ever made more revolutionary changes in his mental attitude towards life and art.

At the age of twenty-three, Whitman made his first appearance as an author. In a periodical called *The New World*, New York, November 1842, there appeared what was described as an "original temperance novel,"

FRANKLIN EVANS: OR, THE INEBRIATE

A Tale of the Times by
WALTER WHITMAN

This is written in an insufferable style, stilted, sophomoric, melodramatic, sentimental, turgid, impossible. It sounds like a burlesque on a temperance tract, but it was serious. T. S. Arthur's *Ten Nights in a Bar-room*, a hot favourite with children, is mild and restrained in comparison with *Franklin Evans: The Inebriate*.

In 1850, in a miscellany called *Voices from the Press*, appeared a short story by Whitman, with the fantastic title, *The Tomb Blossoms*. Here the country is praised in contrast to the city, a strange point of view when we remember *Crossing Brooklyn Ferry*. The style of this tale is no better than that of its predecessor.

Meanwhile, Whitman was studying verse-forms and casting about for something by which to attract the attention of the public. For whether he was a genius or a faker, one thing is certain. Never was there a man who so loved publicity. The limelight was as necessary to his personal comfort as water is to a fish. He could not endure obscurity.

Bliss Perry, in his *Life of Whitman*, has pointed out the remarkable similarity between a free-verse poem, *The Lily and the Bee*, by Samuel Warren, published in 1851, and the style of

Leaves of Grass, 1855. It is impossible to avoid the conclusion, that although Whitman did not borrow from Warren, he had read him with profit. The rhythmic prose of the Bible and the rhapsodical pages of Ossian had been familiar to Whitman since childhood. Evidently, he feared that *Leaves of Grass* might be called an imitation of Ossian, for in the notes that he wrote for his own guidance, we find "Don't fall into the Ossianic *by any chance.*"

When *Leaves of Grass* appeared in 1855, Whitman hoped that it would make a sensation-that it would either be greeted as the work of a new and authentic prophet, or that it would become a public scandal. To his dismay, it fell flat, and attracted hardly any attention. He therefore wrote long and laudatory reviews of it, which appeared anonymously in various periodicals. But even these puffs failed to start a fire.

Whitman sent out presentation copies to distinguished men, and in one instance the result was magnificent. On 21 July 1855, Emerson wrote a glowing and generous letter, that filled the new poet with natural and justifiable exultation. Here are some of the phrases in which Emerson expressed his recognition and tribute. "I find it the most extraordinary piece of wit and wisdom that America has yet contributed. I am very happy in reading it, as great power makes us happy. . . . I find incomparable things, said incomparably well, as they must be I greet you at the beginning of a great career." This last phrase, Whitman, without asking permission, placed in letters of gold, signed R. W.

Emerson, on the outside of the cover of the new edition in 1856, which gave the philosopher the severest test of his tranquillity that he had ever been forced to meet.

Many short reviews of the book consigned it to the garbage-heap, and some insisted that the author should be arrested. Thus there began that fierce quarrel about *Leaves of Grass* that will never be completely and finally settled. The reason is simple enough; there are poems of amazing originality and beauty, and there are passages which never should have been printed.

Whitman was a man of genius; but he had no humour, no taste, and no sense of proportion. On this whole question young Mr. Stevenson, in 1878, said the last word:

> In his desire to accept all facts, facts loyally and simply, it fell within his programme to speak at some length and with some plainness on what is, for I really do not know what reason, the most delicate of subjects. Seeing in that one of the most serious and interesting parts of life, he was aggrieved that it should be looked upon as ridiculous or shameful. No one speaks of maternity with his tongue in his cheek; and Whitman made a bold push to set the sanctity of fatherhood beside the sanctity of motherhood, and introduce this also among the things that can be spoken of without a blush or a wink. But the Philistines have been too strong; and, to say truth, Whitman has rather played the fool. We may be thoroughly conscious that his end is improving; that it would be a good thing if a window were opened on these close privacies of life; that on this subject as on all others, he now and then lets fall a pregnant saying. But we are not satisfied. We feel that he was not the man for so difficult an enterprise. He loses our sympathy in the character of a poet by attracting too much of our attention in that of a Bull in a China Shop. And where, by a little more art, we might have been solemnized ourselves, it is too often Whitman himself alone who is solemn in the face of an audience somewhat indecorously amused.

In dismissing this subject, there is no doubt that Whitman was sincere. But there is also no doubt that his chronic itch for publicity made him more daring than would otherwise have been the case. Since we know how intensely he loved to attract attention, that the chief delight in his life was to be talked about, it is as certain as anything can be that he deliberately put in passages which he believed would make a sensation. They certainly eventually helped to sell his book; they help to sell it now. Emerson pleaded with him in vain; Whitman insisted that nothing should be struck out, and that no abridged version of his poems should appear. Shortly before his death, he finally consented to the publication of a volume of *Selected Poems*, chosen with great skill by Arthur Stedman, who said in his preface, "This edition of Mr. Whitman's poems is, on his part, a concession to friendship.

He has not abandoned his position but has yielded to urgent request." Mr. Stedman did the old poet a valuable service. Those who had heard of Whitman only as a charlatan or as an immoral writer, found in this little volume of Selections enough authentic poetry to change their attitude.

It was not long before parodies appeared, for the subject invited that form of criticism which can best be expressed in parody and burlesque. Whoever is interested in this branch of Whitmania, may now be referred to a book published in 1923, called *Parodies on Walt Whitman*, edited by Henry S. Saunders, with a disarming preface by Christopher Morley. The parodies begin with the year 1857, and close with 1921. Most of them do not seem nearly so funny to us as they must have seemed to their authors. The times have changed, and Whitman is an accepted poet. His peculiarities are so well known that the parody now fails of its intended effect. The best one in the book, as might be expected, is that by the late H. C. Bunner.

The reason why, with a few exceptions like Emerson, *Leaves of Grass* was received either with silence or with abuse, was because of its unlikeness to conventional poetry. When genius supplies a demand, as in the instances of Byron and Tennyson, immediate popularity is the result. There has always been, there is now, and there always will be, a sharp demand for beautifully melodious poetry. But where Genius has to create the demand as well as the supply, where the new forms or the new treatment are entirely unlike what the world is looking for, then the way towards recognition is difficult. Original genius is outside of the law of supply and demand. There was no demand for Browning, or for Ibsen, or for Wagner, or for Whitman; these four men had to create the demand as well as the supply. The mass of people are conventional, like schoolboys, and they distrust and often hate anything that is unconventional or even unusual. What first impressed the public in the works of these Four was not its greatness, but its *strangeness*; that quality of strangeness had to overcome the natural opposition and inertia of humanity, before the greatness could be recognised. For the conventional public opinion, as expressed in print hundreds of times on these four men, was, that whatever they might be, they were assuredly not what they professed to be. Ibsen was not a dramatist; Wagner was not a musician; Browning and Whitman were not poets.

How fortunate it was for these four that they all lived to be old! Had they died in middle life, they would have died unrecognised. But Wagner, Ibsen, Browning, and Whitman received in old age the tribute of universal fame, which must have been all the sweeter for having been long deferred.

Yet although Whitman died a famous poet, his reputation then was nothing to what it is now. In the 'nineties, the controlling voice in English poetry was Rudyard Kipling, who was as unlike Whitman as could be imagined. Kipling had vitality, originality, and force; but he expressed himself carefully in conventional metres. The whole tendency of verse in both England and in America then seemed towards more rather than less restraint in form; the most popular poet in America, James Whitcomb Riley, was conventional metrically. He despised Whitman and all his works.

Furthermore, although Whitman's admirers insisted that he was the voice of democracy, the common people never heard him gladly. The average Americans read Longfellow and Whittier, because those poets best expressed their own inarticulate feelings; they knew little about Whitman and cared less. He, the poet of democracy, was read chiefly by a few literary aristocrats in Europe and in America, whose jaded taste required something new.

But owing to the renaissance of poetry which began in Europe and in America a few years before the Great War, and was definitely stimulated by that catastrophe, the general public began to read Whitman, and for the first time, he became a popular poet. Again, a renaissance of poetry necessarily means experimentation; and during the last ten years many young poets are avowed followers of Whitman, both in writing free verse, and in their fondness for new forms of expression. In a word, Whitman has come into his own.

It is perhaps natural that in the nineteenth century Whitman had more admirers in Europe than in America. He was regarded as the poet of Democracy, America's authentic voice. We, who lived in the atmosphere and environment which he tried to express, would not naturally have been so impressed as those dwelling afar off. Europeans have always been trying to find someone who should reveal the American spirit, and many thought the search was rewarded in *Leaves of Grass*.

When discussion of Whitman became common in England, there arose the same violent difference of opinion as was evident here. Dante Rossetti, in a letter to William Allingham in April 1856, wrote, "I have not been so happy in loathing anything for a long while-except, I think, *Leaves of Grass*, by that Orson of yours. I should like just to have the writing of a valentine to him in one of the reviews." Later, in 1878, in commenting on his brother's *Lives of Famous Poets*, Dante Rossetti said: "I am sorry to see that name winding up a summary of great poets." The two brothers never agreed about this, for in 1869, William Michael Rossetti wrote, "That glorious man Whitman will one day be known as one of the greatest sons of Earth, a few steps below Shakespeare on the throne of immortality." Swinburne's opinion about Whitman suffered a curious change. When he first read *Leaves of Grass*, shortly after its appearance, he was enthusiastic and spoke highly of it. Even as late as 1885 he wrote, "I retain a very cordial admiration for not a little of Whitman's earlier work." But in 1887 Swinburne made a thorough recantation, saying that Whitman's Muse was a "drunken apple-woman, indecently sprawling in the slush and garbage of the gutter amid the rotten refuse of her overturned fruit-stall."

In America, Dartmouth College can claim the honour of being the first academic institution to treat Whitman officially with respect. He was invited to deliver the Commencement Poem in 1872, and he accepted, writing and reading on that occasion a poem originally called *As a Strong Bird on Pinions Free.* In the *Complete Works* this title was changed to *Thou Mother with Thy Equal Brood.* In the same year of its delivery he published the Dartmouth poem, with a preface so important, and made even more so by the years 1914-1918, that it is necessary to quote from it.

> The impetus and ideas urging me, for some years past,
> to an utterance, or attempt at utterance, of New World
> songs, and an epic of Democracy, having already had their
> publish'd expression, as well as I can expect to give it, in
> *"Leaves of Grass,"* the present and any future pieces from
> me are really but the surplusage forming after that volume,
> or the wake eddying behind it. I fulfill'd in that an imperi-
> ous conviction, and the commands of my nature as total
> and irresistible as those which make the sea flow, or the
> globe revolve. But of this supplementary volume, I confess
>
> I am not so certain. Having from early manhood
> abandon'd the business pursuits and applications usual
> in my time and country, and obediently yielded myself
> up ever since to the impetus mention'd, and to the work
> of expressing those ideas, it may be that mere habit has
> got dominion of me, when there is no real need of say-
> ing anything further. But what is life but an experiment?
> and mortality but an exercise? with reference to results
> beyond. And so shall my poems be. If incomplete here,

and superfluous there, n'importe-the earnest trial and persistent exploration shall at least be mine, and other success failing shall be success enough. I have been more anxious, anyhow, to suggest the songs of vital endeavour and manly evolution, and furnish something for races of outdoor athletes, than to make perfect rhymes, or reign in the parlours. I ventur'd from the beginning my own way, taking chances-and would keep on venturing.

I will therefore not conceal from any persons, known or unknown to me, who take an interest in the matter, that I have the ambition of devoting yet a few years to poetic composition. The mighty present age! To absorb and express in poetry, anything of it-of its world-America-cities and States-the years, the events of our Nineteenth century-the rapidity of movement, the violent contrasts, fluctuations of light and shade, of hope, and fear-the entire revolution made by science in the poetic method-these great new underlying facts and new ideas rushing and spreading everywhere; truly a mighty age! As if in some colossal drama, acted again like those of old under the open sun, the Nations of our time, and all the characteristics of Civilization, seem hurrying, stalking across, flitting from wing to wing, gathering, closing up, towards some long prepared, most tremendous denouement. Not to conclude the infinite scenes of the race's life and toil and happiness and sorrow, but haply that the boards be cleared from oldest, worst incumbrances, accumulations, and Man resume the eternal play anew, and under happier, free, auspices. To me, the United States are important because in this colossal drama they are unquestionably designated for the leading parts, for many a century to come. In them history and humanity seem to seek to culminate. Our broad areas are even now the busy theatre of plots, passions, interest, and suspended problems, compared to which the intrigues

of the past of Europe, the wars of dynasties, the scope of
kings and kingdoms, and even the development of peoples,
as hitherto, exhibit scales of measurement comparatively
narrow and trivial. And on these areas of ours, as on a
stage, sooner or later, something like an *eclaircissement* of
all the past civilization of Europe and Asia is probably to
be evolved.

The leading parts. Not to be acted, emulated here, by us
again, that role till now foremost in history-not to become
a conqueror nation, or to achieve the glory of mere mili-
tary, or diplomatic, or commercial superiority-but to be-
come the grand producing land of nobler men and women
-of copious races, cheerful, healthy, tolerant, free-to be-
come the most friendly nation (the United States, indeed)-
the modern composite nation, form'd from all, with room
for all, welcoming all immigrants-accepting the work of
our own interior development, as the work fitly filling ages
and ages to come;-the leading nation of peace, but neither
ignorant nor incapable of being the leading nation of war;
not the man's nation only, but the woman's nation-a land
of splendid mothers, daughters, sisters, wives. . . .

The Four Years' War is over-and in the peaceful, strong,
exciting, fresh occasions of to-day, and of the future, that
strange, sad war is hurrying even now to be forgotten.
The camp, the drill, the lines of sentries, the prisons, the
hospitals- (ah! the hospitals!)-all have passed away-all
seem now like a dream. A new race, a young and lusty
generation, already sweeps in with oceanic currents,
obliterating the war, and all its scars, its mounded graves,
and all its reminiscences of hatred, conflict, death. So let
it be obliterated. I say the life of the present and the future
makes undeniable demands upon us each and all, south,
north, east, west. To help put the United States (even if

only in imagination) hand in hand, in one unbroken circle in a chant-to rouse them to the unprecedented grandeur of the part they are to play, and are even now playing-to the thought of their great future, and the attitude conform'd to it-especially their great esthetic, moral, scientific future (of which their vulgar material and political present is but as the preparatory tuning of instruments by an orchestra), these, as hitherto, are still, for me, among my hopes, ambitions.

How far and in what sense is Whitman an original writer? It is often stated that he is one of our most original thinkers and poets. His leading ideas are not original. He expresses chiefly enthusiasm for humanity, love of the race, the worship of democracy; all this is emphatically and at times impressively uttered. But it can be found in Rousseau and has been more poetically expressed by Shelley. Has then Whitman nothing new or important to tell us? He says "Rejoice in yourselves: in life: in all your bodily functions." Had he proclaimed this some centuries earlier, he might have been called original. The revolt against asceticism, the refusal to regard the human body as vile, the unwillingness to consider human life on earth as a mere vestibule to eternity these are fundamental ideas in Whitman. But he was by no means the first to proclaim them.

I should say that Whitman was more unconventional than original. As he discarded fashionable clothing, so he discarded fashionable opinions. In America he was more "different" than he would have seemed in Europe. Here he was against the Puritan tradition, against what was understood and agreed upon as decency, against small-town mentality, against any and all reserve. His manners shocked Americans as they could not have shocked Europeans; for example, he was forever kissing men, which simply "isn't done" in America. I remember when a European pianist played in Boston, he was entertained after the concert by an exclusive club. He caused a sensation by insisting on kissing every one of the men who were presented to him. It took them a long while to recover.

Much of the shock caused by Whitman's poetry really had more to do with literary etiquette than with thought. It was largely a question of manners. Now the older a civilisation is, the freer and franker the behaviour and conversation of the people. In the nineteenth century, things were discussed in books and at dinner-tables on the Continent which were never mentioned in America. And what is true of an old country as compared with a new is true of a large city as compared with a village. Country bumpkins will snigger secretly over vulgarities; but village society says limb when it means leg; prefers circumlocutions to direct statements; and still prefers rhetorical oratory to simple plain language. It is the last citadel of the old-fashioned spell-binder.

In the same way, old countries are more tolerant of religious and political heresies than new ones; and in any country, there is more freedom of speech in a big city than in a village. During and after the Great War, there was more individual freedom of speech in England than in America; and in America, there was more freedom in New York than anywhere else, much more than in country villages. Many were surprised that the penalties - twenty years in prison, for example - that were given to persons who expressed heretical political opinions in America were unknown in England; this is really natural, and is simply a register of intellectual levels. We had and have the small-town view, that cannot comprehend opinions contrary to those current in the village.

Whitman's lack of reserve on all topics and his unconventionalities were startling in America in 1855.

In one respect he had the wisdom of the great poets. He was never an opportunist; he did not deal with "timely" questions. Though intensely American, as a poet he was universal and dealt with universal and unchangeable things like human passions and the stars. He was a revolutionist in art, but he was never a political revolutionist; he was not a socialist, not an anarchist, not a political reformer. He was kept from all this not only by his intense individualism, which would have made it impossible for him to cooperate with any organisation, but by a kind of instinctive wisdom, which made him deal with fundamental and eternal things, the true subjects of art.

Whitman's religion was certainly not Christianity, except in one important aspect, his belief in the brotherhood of man. Not only was he devoid even of a grain of Christian faith, he was definitely in opposition to Christian teaching. If I understand Christianity at all, it is opposed to human instincts; it proposes to substitute unselfishness for selfishness, modesty for greed, purity for sensuality, giving for taking, self-control for self-assertion. The reason why Christianity is so unpopular at the present moment-for unpopular it certainly is-is not because it is opposed to reason, for it is in harmony with the only reasonable way of life. It is unpopular because it places a constant veto on human instincts, and we are living (1923) in a post-war relaxation and hatred of all restraint. Possibly one reason why Christianity has never been popular in any period with the younger generation is because early in life instinct is stronger than reason; wisdom comes, if at all, by experience. Christianity is of course a positive, not a negative religion; it is a religion to live by, not to die by; but, as Browning said, it teaches original sin, the corruption of man's heart. Christianity never uses palliatives or surface remedies; it calls for regeneration, for a new birth, for a complete change in emphasis.

Keats said in one of his letters, "O for a life of sensations rather than of thoughts!" Whitman is more of a sensationalist than a thinker. The tentacles of his mind were all feelers; he was like an Aeolian harp, to be played upon by the chance winds of heaven. To regard him as a profound philosopher, prophet, or great teacher is idle; he shows us how to enjoy life, how to appreciate beauty, how to become ever more sensitive to impressions, but he very seldom stimulates the mind. Professor Henry A. Beers is very near the final truth about him, when he says, "If a large, good-natured, clean, healthy animal could write poetry, it would write such poetry as the *Leaves of Grass*. It would tell how good it is to lie and bask in the warm sun; to stand in cool, flowing water, to be naked in the fresh air; to troop with friendly companions and to embrace one's mate."

One of the reasons why Whitman is so popular at this moment is because many of our novelists and men of letters have substituted the animal for the spiritual attitude towards life. We used to be told that we should conquer the beast in us; now we are told every day to imitate the animals, to be like them, do what we please, and never on any account be sorry afterwards. There are many prominent writers to-day to whom the word sin is obsolete. They are, consciously or unconsciously, followers of Whitman. I cannot imagine old Walt suffering from anything like remorse.

So far as he had a religion, he can be described by the well-known phrase, "cosmic emotion," concerning which Professor W. K. Clifford wrote an interesting essay. Man must have some religion or some substitute for religion; I do not believe the average human being can live without it. If all theistic belief is dead, the religion of nature remains. One goes out at night, contemplates the stars, and feels oneself a part of the universe. To Whitman this was always a solemnizing thought. "The huge and thoughtful night." He was sincere in what religion he had. When a dying soldier asked Whitman to read him a chapter in the New Testament, he read the account of the crucifixion. "The poor wasted young man ask'd me to read the following chapter also, how Christ rose again. I read very slowly, for Oscar was feeble. It pleased him very much, yet the tears were in his eyes. He ask'd me if I enjoyed religion. I said, 'Perhaps not, my dear, in the way you mean, and yet, maybe, it is the same thing.' He said, 'It is my chief reliance.' He talk'd of death, and said he did not fear it."

Whitman was a careful student of rhythm and had read the Bible to advantage. His best lines have superb rolling music that needs no rime, although he did not disdain rime. His most famous poem is also the most conventional in metre, "O Captain, My Captain." Whitman became tired of hearing this praised, both because he did not wish to be regarded as a man of one poem, and because it was so unlike his more characteristic work. When someone praised it one day, he exclaimed angrily, "Oh, *damn* My Captain!" His impatience is easy to understand. We are told that a man voted against Aristides because he was tired of hearing him called The Just, but think how utterly weary Aristides himself must have been.

I hold no brief for free verse; other things being equal, I prefer regular metrical forms. But there are certain subjects, which, if Whitman had described them in sonnets, could not have been so impressively brought to our perceptions as Whitman brings them with his irregularities. Take the lines he wrote in Platte Canon, Colorado.

> *Spirit that form'd this scene,*
> *These tumbled rock-piles grim and red,*
> *These reckless heaven-ambitious peaks,*
> *These gorges, turbulent-clear streams, this naked freshness,*
> *These formless wild arrays, for reasons of their own,*
> *I know thee, savage spirit-we have communed together,*
> *Mine too such wild arrays, for reasons of their own;*
> *Was't charged against my chants they had forgotten art?*
> *To fuse within themselves its rules precise and delicatesse?*
> *The lyrist's measur'd beat, the wrought-out temple's grace-*
>   *column and polish'd arch forgot?*
> *But thou that revelest here-spirit that form'd this scene,*
> *They have remembered thee.*

Although Whitman has an unassailable place in literature, and although he has profoundly influenced many young poets, and at no time more than now, his own method-free verse-has not yet given birth to anything supreme. The best free-verse writing in the English language is still to be found in Whitman, and not in the works of his imitators or followers. They have done well, but not supremely well; and their best is below the best conventional work done by their contemporaries. Whitman was undoubtedly a great poet; but who are the leading English poets of the twentieth century? Kipling, Thompson, Phillips, Housman, Henley, Hardy, Hodgson, De La Mare, Noyes, Masefield, Watson, Brooke, Flecker, Davies; and in America, our three leading living poets are Robinson, Lindsay, and Frost. Neither in England nor in America are the leaders distinguished for free verse composition, but rather for the opposite. Therefore the old battle-cry, that Whitman's is "the poetry of the future," seems particularly untrue.

There are still those who would deny Whitman the rank of great poet. But we should remember that the Republic of Letters is not a social club; genius cannot be blackballed, and Whitman was a man of genius. He often expressed a universal idea in a permanently beautiful phrase. His greatness, indeed, consists not so much in whole poems as in phrases. He had a particular talent for first lines and titles, so that the Table of Contents or Index of First Lines to Whitman's Complete Poems would seem full of promise to one who should stumble on the book without previous knowledge. Like some grocers, he put the best apples on top. Looking down the *Table of Contents*, one feels that the Table itself is a Poem.

In Cabin'd Ships at Sea
I Hear America Singing
Shut not Your Doors to Me, Proud Libraries
Out of the Rolling Ocean the Crowd
Once I Pass'd Through a Populous City
I Heard You Solemn-Sweet Pipes of the Organ
When I Heard at the Close of the Day
I Saw in Louisiana a Live-Oak Growing
This Moment Yearning and Thoughtful

Fast-Anchored Eternal O Love
O You Whom I Often and Silently Come
Song of the Open Road
Song of the Redwood Tree
Song of the Rolling Earth
Youth, Day, Old Age, and Night
Pioneers! O Pioneers!
Out of the Cradle Endlessly Rocking
As I Ebb'd With the Ocean of Life
To the Man-of-War Bird
The World Below the Brine
On the Beach at Night Alone
Song for All Seas, All Ships
When I Heard the Learn'd Astronomer
The Dalliance of the Eagles
Beat! Beat! Drums!
From Paumanok Starting I Fly Like a Bird
Song of the Banner at Daybreak
Rise O Days from Your Fathomless Deeps
Cavalry Crossing a Ford
By the Bivouac's Fitful Flame
Vigil Strange I Kept on the Field One Night
A Sight in Camp in the Daybreak Gray and Dim
As Toilsome I wander'd Virginia's Woods
Year that Trembled and Reel'd Beneath Me
Give Me the Splendid Silent Sun
Over the Carnage Rose Prophetic a Voice
I Saw Old General at Bay
Ethiopia Saluting the Colors
O Tan-Faced Prairie-Boy
Look Down Fair Moon
When Lilacs Last in the Dooryard Bloom'd
O Captain, My Captain
Hush'd be the Camps To-day
By Blue Ontario's Shore

There was a Child Went Forth
The Singer in the Prison
Warble for Lilac-Time
O Star of France
An Old Man's Thought of School
Proud Music of the Storm
Prayer of Columbus
Darest Thou Now O Soul
Yet, Yet, Ye Downcast Hours
As if a Phantom Caress'd Me
That Music Always Round Me
A Noiseless Patient Spider
Thou Mother with Thy Equal Brood
Thou Orb Aloft Full-Dazzling
The Mystic Trumpeter
To a Locomotive in Winter
Ah Poverties, Wincings, and Sulky Retreats
Weave in, My Hardy Life
By Broad Potomac's Shore
From Far Dakota's Canons
Spirit That Form'd this Scene
As I Walk These Broad Majestic Days
The Sobbing of the Bells
Joy, Shipmate, Joy
Sands at Seventy
Good-By, My Fancy

The art of poetry is an art of expression; we are all poets at heart. We all have imagination and poetic thought, else why should we find in the great poets so clear an echo of ourselves? The more distinct the echo, the greater the poet. But we are inarticulate; we cannot express ourselves; we love music, and we cannot sing. The great poets are the spokesmen for humanity. Whitman spoke out for us all. There are passages in such poems as *Columbus, When Lilacs Last, The Man-of-War Bird*, that rhythmically sing thoughts that are universal.

Furthermore, there is something healthy in his optimism. He was never petulant, never cynical, never despairing. To him Life was good. He belongs not among those who have despised the supreme gift of life, not among the deniers, but among the Affirmers. He was entirely free from the prevailing modern disease, the fear of life. He loved life and welcomed experience; he was devoid of fear. He calls upon us to rejoice; to use our eyes and our senses; to commune in rapture with the sea and the stars.

In a certain sense, Whitman interpreted America to Europe; and to America he tried to interpret the universe.

www.ingramcontent.com/pod-product-compliance
Lightning Source LLC
Chambersburg PA
CBHW051742040426

42447CB00008B/1263